YOU'LL LOVE THIS STUFF!

poems from many cultures

selected by
MORAG STYLES

Illustrations by Bernard Georges

CAMBRIDGE UNIVERSITY PRESS

Cambridge

London   New York   New Rochelle

Melbourne   Sydney

for Keith

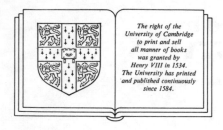

Published by the Press Syndicate of the University of Cambridge
The Pitt Building, Trumpington Street, Cambridge CB2 1RP
32 East 57th Street, New York, NY 10022, USA
10 Stamford Road, Oakleigh, Melbourne 3166, Australia

First published 1986

Printed in Great Britain at the University Press, Cambridge

ISBN 0 521 32130 1 hard covers
ISBN 0 521 31275 2 paperback

GE

Contents

An asterisk indicates that the poem has been written by a young person.

For Parents and Teachers

You'll Love This Stuff and *I Like That Stuff*, its companion volume, share the same aims and intentions. They are both explorations of poetry suitable for children all over the world.

In Britain most anthologies for children concentrate on English poetry with a smattering from U.S.A, Japan, Australia and one or two other countries. We do have a fine tradition of poetry written for children in Britain and many contemporary poets have opened up new forms and styles of writing with great appeal to children. But we are now living in a multiethnic society and this should be reflected in the literature we present to children. And we are denying all our children, if we do not offer them the widest possible variety of poetry in childhood. *You'll Love This Stuff* and *I Like That Stuff* attempt some redressing of the balance. As well as drawing on poetry from different cultures, I have given prominence to black British poets who are not yet as widely known as they deserve to be. Otherwise, I have deliberately avoided popular English poets who are already much anthologised.

The Caribbean with its vigorous oral tradition was, perhaps, the liveliest source of poetic material outside Britain. Although there are many fine Caribbean poets writing in standard English (A.L. Hendriks for example), I have tended to focus on dialect poetry for its vitality and humour. This poetry comes alive when read aloud. The glossary at the end may help those who are new to dialect poetry.

The African continent was also rich in possibilities from its oral as well as its written forms. The more spiritual and philosophical bent of Indian literature made it less accessible, but I was pleased to come up with poems, both ancient and modern, with appeal for children. Chinese and Japanese poetry both have much to offer children, especially in terms of the brevity and simplicity of poetic expression. I continued my research through Europe, Scandinavia, the Far East, finding an abundance of good poetry. On the whole, I chose poems which would not be familiar to children, but the occasional 'old favourite' was impossible to resist. In an anthology such as this, it is inevitable that a high proportion of the poetry is translated. These have been carefully selected with different versions compared whenever possible. Naturally, something is lost, but with good translations, something is gained as well.

Despite reading so much diverse poetry from all over the world, old and new, serious and strange, whimsical and hilarious, I made the obvious discovery that across the seas and the centuries so much is *similar*. Poets writing with children in mind chose the timeless themes of family life, pleasures, disappointments, animals, humour and, of course, themselves, whenever or wherever they lived.

There are quite a number of poems written by young people in both anthologies. I enjoy the freshness of their voices, their honesty. It is interesting that most of the poems in the section entitled 'At School Today' were by children. They certainly give schools and teachers a hard time! This was not intentional, but just how it happened to work out.

The other sections fell naturally into place from my collection. I found many poems about hunting and the hunted, the animals that have not been domesticated, so that was an obvious grouping for 'Wild Life'. Poems about babies and children, parents and grandparents slotted into 'Babes in Arms'. Poems relating to the sea, rivers, streams, the rain, fish and fishermen made up 'Water Water Everywhere'. An assortment of fun of various kinds led to 'Play Time'. The section that excited me most was 'Of Poets I Speak' because it was so unexpected to discover so many wonderful poems on poetry itself.

I believe that poetry is very important to children who have an intuitive feel for its rhyme, rhythm and repetitions, especially in early childhood. These anthologies attempt to harness and exploit this early pleasure in word play, and to develop and enrich this instinct for poetry which is in every child. Apart from the Caribbean dialect glossary, I make no attempt to teach or explain, but leave the poems to do their own work. There is plenty here that is amusing and reassuring, but there are also poems to challenge. Experience has taught me not to underestimate children. Good poetry works on a level of inner understanding for the individual which is not necessarily improved by analysis.

I hope this anthology offers something for all children with its variety of themes, forms and uses of language. *You'll Love This Stuff* is, finally, a celebration of the common humanity we all share. If it interests, excites, surprises, amuses and, above all, delights the reader, I shall be well satisfied.

Morag Styles

Listen

Shhhhhhhhhhhhhhhhhhhhhhhhhhh!
Sit still, very still
And listen.
Listen to wings
Lighter than eyelashes
Stroking the air.
Know what the thin breeze
Whispers on high
To the cocunut trees.
Listen and hear.

Telcine Turner
Bahamas

Babes in Arms

It is not difficult
to fill a child's hand.

from the Ashanti
Translated by R.S. Rattray
West Africa

Tiger wahn to eat a child,
tiger sey he could swear it was a puss!

James Berry
Jamaica/U.K.

1.   The sun is rising,
At either side a bow is lying,
Beside the bows are lion-babies,
The sky is pink,
     That is all.

The moon is setting,
At cither side are bamboos for arrow-making,
Beside the bamboos are wild cat babies,
They walk uncertainly,
     That is all.

from the Papago
Translated by F. Densmore
American Indian

Nonsense Lullaby

Baby swimming down the river,
Driftwood leggies, rabbit leggies,
  Little rabbit leggies.

from the Kiowa
Translated by N. Curtis
American Indian

Sleep, little one, sleep.
Why are his ears so long?
Baby rabbit of Sleepy Hill?
When his mother carried him
She ate acorns, mulberries.
That is why his ears
Have grown so very long.

traditional
Translated by G. Bownas and A. Thwaite
Japan

Paddling Song

My dugout canoe goes
Swiftly down the river.
In every tree the monkeys
Are chattering and crying.
Oh, big jungle hunter,
Tell me of their trouble.

The little monkey broke his leg,
So they are all crying.

Then bend to your paddle,
Hunter of the river,
And tell the mother that
Her monkey-baby's crying.
The little monkey broke his leg.
They are all crying.

from the Bantu
Translated by M. Exner
Southern Africa

Wandering Breezes

The catkins line the lanes,
    making white carpets,
And leaves on lotus streams
    spread like green money:

Pheasants root bamboo shoots,
    nobody looking,
While ducklings on the sands
    sleep by their mothers.

Tu Fu
800 A.D.
Translated by A. Cooper
China

A Day Like Any Other

A day like any other. Memory dozed. A chilly
and dreary spring dragged on. Then, all at once,
a shadow at the bottom stirred
and from the bottom rose with sobs.

What's there to sob about? I'm a poor soother!
Yet how she stamps her feet, and shakes and hotly
clings to my neck and in the dreadful darkness
begs to be gathered up, as babes are, in one's arms.

Vladimir Nabokov
Russia/U.S.A.

Little Flower

Your arrival was unplanned
unscheduled, you burst
into the afternoon of
our already mapped-out lives

and Life was chaos
for a short while . . .
We had to shift beds
rearrange the furniture
to accommodate you
tiny stranger from nowhere

But it was worthwhile
already you illuminate
our humdrum mornings
with your gurgling smile
bubbly companion to your brother
little flower that blossomed in late October.

Cecil Rajendra
Malaysia

Transformations

My little son enters
the room and says
'You are a vulture
I am a mouse'

I put away my book
wings and claws
grow out of me
their ominous shadows
race on the walls
I am a vulture
he is a mouse

'You are a wolf
I am a goat'
I walked round the table
and am a wolf
windowpanes gleam
like fangs
in the dark

while he runs to his mother
safe
his head hidden in the warmth of her dress

Tadeusz Różewicz
Translated by C. Milosz
Poland

12

Luchin

Fragile as a kite over the roofs of Barrancas,
little Luchin was playing,
his hands blue with cold,
with his rag ball,
the cat and the dog . . .
and the horse looked on.

His eyes brimming pools of green,
his brief life spent crawling,
little bare bottom in the mud.

The horse was another toy for him
in that tiny space,
and it seemed that the horse enjoyed his job,
with the rag ball,
the cat and the dog,
and Luchin wet through.

If there are children like Luchin
who eat earth and worms,
let's open their cages,
so that they can fly away like birds,

with the rag ball,
the cat and the dog
and with the horse too.

Victor Jara
Chile

**Questions I couldn't answer when
asked by my four-year old nephew . . .**

i.   Why doesn't the river flow sidewise
       – bank to bank – ?

ii.   If 1 plus 1 is 2
       & two plus two makes 4

       how come 0 plus 0 is always zero?

iii.   What do the eyes of a bubble see?

iv.   little daisies
       little lotuses
       little arches of rainbows
       &
       little birds
       little animals
       little oceans
       &
       little mountains
       &
       little people
       why didn't god make the world that way?

v.   Who is lonelier – the sun or the moon?

vi.   If all of us talked in songs
       & not in words

       would we still be fighting?

vii.   Why must everything die, Badbaba?

Deba Patnaik
India

Seville Slumber Song

This little scallawag
does not have a mother;
gypsy gave birth to him,
threw him in the street.
Has no mother, yes,
has no mother, no,
ain't got no mother, she
threw him in the street.

This tiny fellow
does not have a cradle;
his father is a carpenter
& will make him one.

Federico Garcia Lorca
Translated by Paul Blackburn
Spain

Ayo

her name
was Ayo

and as
she smiled

I saw teeth
white as ivory

but she was
more precious
than all the
ivory in Africa

Eugene Perkins
U.S.A.

Stars

Near the book a notebook
near the notebook a glass
near the glass a child
in the child's hand a cat.
And far away stars stars.

Oktay Rifat
Translated by K. Bosley
Turkey

Consistently Ignored

Consistently ignored in a family of ten
I asked mother, 'Am I your real son?'
She paused from grinding spice,
'No, I bought you from a beggar
For a bushel of rice!'
From behind sisters giggled.

I matched features, spied on beggars
Roamed the backyard thinking
Of distant huts, certain
My mother sat busy in one
Scheming to trade another son
For fish to add to that bushel.

G. S. Sharat Chandra
India

A Young Lady's Horoscope

You'll be rich – or you'll be poor.
You'll store meat for the New Year.
Of your parents, one is male
and the other is female.
When you marry, your baby
will be a girl – or a boy.

traditional
Translated by K. Bosley
Vietnam

My Papa's Waltz

The whisky on your breath
Could make a small boy dizzy;
But I hung on like death:
Such waltzing was not easy.

We romped until the pans
Slid from the kitchen shelf;
My mother's countenance
Could not unfrown itself.

The hand that held my wrist
Was battered on one knuckle;
At every step you missed
My right ear scraped a buckle.

You beat time on my head
With a palm caked hard by dirt,
Then waltzed me off to bed
Still clinging to your shirt.

Theodore Roethke
U.S.A.

from **Mother**

She lived in a lonely village.
All day she worked at home, silently.
Hardly noticed the sun
throbbing in a summer sky
and rafts of clouds sailing by.
She did not notice time moving on.

Everything was familiar:
painted in gentle colours,
an intricate pattern woven carefully.
A pot of boiling rice, greens,
some fish: a plebeian meal
for her husband, a schoolteacher.

At times she would glance
at the creepers near the fence
or at the yellow bird on the jackfruit tree
wagging its tail endlessly.
And time would move on.

A quick bath by the well
and she would comb her greying tresses
thinking of her son
in the local school
memorising multiplication tables.
She would think of her eldest son,
as she wrapped the jar with sweets
in pretty wrappings . . .
his large bright eyes
the city in which he studied.

Her footfalls would never be heard
outside this small world of her own:
she would never venture out.
It was a self-imposed exile:
a simple life of her own.

Shamsur Rahman
Translated by P. Nandy
Bangladesh

Children's Song

Huge snowflakes dancing down,
Great hailstones spattering.
At the back door
Dumplings are boiling,
Red beans are seething.
The hunter is now returning,
The baby is howling,
And I can't find the ladle –
What a life, what a life!

traditional
Translated by G. Bownas & A. Thwaite
Japan

When You're No Longer A Child

You know you're not a child anymore
When your mum and dad stop saying, 'Time for bed',
When you're expected to help with the housework,
When 'O-Levels' loom,
When you understand the meaning of death,
When you think about getting a job,
When people talk to you about responsibility,
When Jackanory loses its magic,
When you stop playing cowboys and Indians
Then you are an adult.

Mark Ludwig*
U.K.

My Grandfather in Cyprus

I'd like to meet my grandad
But he lives in a land far away,
Where it is hot and sunny.
I hear he is an old man now,
His face is wrinkled like a lemon in the sun.
When we meet
We will talk in Greek,
Someday.

Michael Xenofontos*
U.K.

24

Bed-Time Story

Ah long fi see yuh tell ah short!
Whe yuh deh all dis time?
Dah pickininni yah woan go sleep,
She waan me tell her rhyme.

Mary had a little lamb
– Miss Mattie li bwoy Joe
Go kick May slap pon har doorway –
His feet was white as snow.

An everywhere dat Mary went
– Him modder never know,
And when she ear she ongle seh –
De lamb was sure to go.

She ongle seh de bwoy too bad
An tell May nuffi bawl
– *Jack and Jill went up de hill* –
An dat was all an all.

May mighta go to hospital
– *To catch a pail of water;*
Jack fell down an bruck his crown –
Jus like Miss Mattie daughter.

Yuh never know de baby bawn?
Him pa gi him name Marta.
Teng God him drop eento a doze
– *An Jill come tumblin after.*

Louise Bennett
Jamaica

Play Time

Don't meddle with muck
or the pigs will eat you.

traditional
Collected by Vasco Popa
Translated by Anne Pennington
Yugoslavia

This creature has ten tongues, twenty eyes, forty feet
and walks with difficulty.
Answer: A sow carrying nine piglets.

traditional
Translated by K. Crossley-Holland
Viking/Scandinavia

How to Say Hello

Kiss a baby
Pat a dog
Stroke a kitten
Scratch a hog
Curtsey to a queen,
Or bow,
Chase a chicken,
Call a cow;
If any other
Thing should greet you
Say 'How do you do?
I'm pleased to meet you.'
(Unless you think
It wants to eat you.)

Dennis Doyle
U.K.

If You Want To See An Alligator

If you want to see an alligator
you must go down to the muddy slushy
end of the old Caroony River

I know an alligator
who's living down there –
She's a-Mean. She's a-Big. She's a-Wicked
She's a-Fierce.

Yes, if you really want to see
an alligator, you must go down to the
muddy slushy end of the old Caroony River

Go down gently to that River and say,
'Alligator Mama
Alligator Mama
Alligator Mamaaaaaaaaaaaa'

And up she'll rise
But don't stick around
RUN FOR YOUR LIFE!

Grace Nichols
Guyana/U.K.

The Spider and the Fly

The spider said to the fly:
'Do look in when you come by.
It will be an honour.
I have a new home, new decor;
See the staircase and the curtains,
And the walls are hung with mirrors.'
The fly hesitated: 'I don't know . . .
I haven't seen anyone going up the stairs
That came down again.' The spider
Then resorted to flattery:
'You are looking absolutely lovely;
Your eyes sparkle like sequins,
and that glittering dress! . . .
I must say you are always busy
washing yourself and humming
As you fly that soothing tune.'
The fly winged past, flattered
That she had a new admirer.
'All right' she said and entered the web.

Mohammed Iqbal
Adapted and translated by Munawar Syed
Pakistan

Anancy

Anancy is a spider;
Anancy is a man;
Anancy's West Indian
And West African.

Sometimes, he wears a waistcoat;
Sometimes, he carries a cane;
Sometimes, he sports a top hat;
Sometimes, he's just a plain,
Ordinary, black, hairy spider.

Anancy is vastly cunnng,
Tremendously greedy,
Excessively charming,
Hopelessly dishonest,
Warmly loving,
Firmly confident,
Fiercely wild,
A fabulous character,
Completely out of our mind
And out of his, too.

Anancy is a master planner,
A great user
Of other people's plans;
He pockets everybody's food,
Shelter, land, money, and more;
He achieves mountains of things,
Like stolen flour dumplings;
He deceives millions of people,
Even the man in the moon;
And he solves all the mysteries
On earth, in air, under sea.

And always,
Anancy changes
From a spider into a man
And from a man into a spider
And back again
At the drop of a sleepy eyelid.

Andrew Salkey
Jamaica

31

It's Fun (for Julian who asked for a dolphin poem)

It's fun
in the sun
and cool
in the pool
with pleasant shadows
to hide away
and I never know need
with a regular feed
at special times every day

But oh to be free
in the wide open sea
roaming the ocean meadows
or to laze in the bay
and gambol all day

To be free, to be free, to be free!

Dennis Brutus
South Africa

My Cat(s)

My Cat(s),
I have 8 of them,
1 stray and 7 wanderers,
Such lazy animals basking in the Sun,
bathing in their glory.
Licking their Summer, stroke Winter coats.
Wanting all the attention,
especially at meal times.
Mother, Queen of the garden,
Father, unknown.
8 different colours
in odd shapes and in
    odd sizes.
All miniature tigers,
Clawing their tender skin,
Snarling at their owner.
Feeling no remorse for one another,
Each man for himself!

Mary D. Chauhan*
U.K.

The Butterfly

I always think the butterfly
Looks best against a clear blue sky;
I do not think he looks so good
Pinned down within a box of wood.

Frank Collymore
Barbados

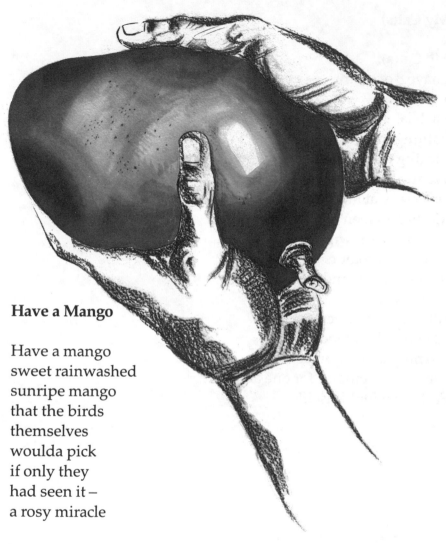

Have a Mango

Have a mango
sweet rainwashed
sunripe mango
that the birds
themselves
woulda pick
if only they
had seen it –
a rosy miracle

Here

take it from mih hand.

Grace Nichols
Guyana/U.K.

from **Dumplin**

It might be fried or boil
Soft or even tough
But dumplin is a ting
You can never get enough.
De sort a dumplin weh me like
Is really hard fe chew
It stick inside me teet
Like it stick wid superglue.
Yuh can eat it wid green banana
Yam an dasheen too
Ackee and some saltfish
Sweet potato and calliloo.
Den me cum to cornmeal dumplin
When someting me did learn
Dat when me eat de cornmeal
It mek me stomach burn.
De next we eat wid breakfast
It's someting we've all tried
Yes it's dat famous dumplin
Dat me call 'Freddie fried'.
A dumplin is tradition
Part of history
To de English it is chips
And a good old cup of tea.
When me see it pon de table
Lyin pon me plate
It's someting dat me love
Dat me will never ever hate.
So when yuh run out of flour
Yuh better start to fret

Because a house wid out a dumplin
Is a house dat I'll forget.
So to those who do not like dem
Who jus can't stand de taste
Dere is nuting you can show me
Dat a dumplin can't replace.

Martin Glyn
U.K.

The Pawpaw

Four little boys, tattered,
Fingers and faces splattered
With mud, had climbed
In the rain and caught
A pawpaw which they brought,
Like a bomb, to my house. I saw
Them coming: a serious, mumbling,
Tumbling bunch who stopped
At the steps in a hunch.
Releasing the fruit from the leaf
It was wrapped in, I watched them
Carefully wash the pawpaw
Like a nugget of gold. This done,
With rainwater, till it shone
They climbed into the house
To present the present to me.
A mocking sign of the doom of all flesh?
Or the purest gold in the kingdom?

Edward Kamau Brathwaite
Barbados

Hi, Coconut

Coconut tree
so tall and high
when I look up at yuh
I got to wink up me eye.

Coconut tree
yuh coconut big
like football in the sky.
Drop down one fo me nuh.

If only I could reach yuh
if only I could reach yuh
is sweet water and jelly
straight to me belly.

But right now coconut
yuh deh up so high
I can't reach yuh
I could only tell yuh,
                    Hi,

          Hi, Coconut

John Agard
Guyana/U.K.

Don' Go Ova Dere

Barry madda tell im
But Barry woudn' hear,
Barry fada warn im
But Barry didn' care.
'Don' go ova dere, bwoy,
Don' go ova dere.'

Barry sista beg im
Barry pull her hair,
Barry brother bet im
'You can't go ova dere.'
'I can go ova dere, bwoy,
I can go ova dere.'

Barry get a big bag,
Barry climb de gate,
Barry granny call im
But Barry couldn' wait,
Im wan' get ova dere, bwoy,
Before it get too late.

Barry see de plum tree
Im didn' see de bull,
Barry thinkin' bout de plums
'Gwine get dis big bag full.'
De bull get up an' shake, bwoy,
An gi de rope a pull.

De rope slip off de pole
But Barry didn' see,
De bull begin to stretch im foot dem
Barry climb de tree.
Barry start fe eat, bwoy,
Firs' one, den two, den three.

Barry nearly full de bag
An den im hear a soun'
Barry hol' de plum limb tight
An start fe look aroun'
When im see de bull, bwoy,
Im nearly tumble down.

Night a come, de bull naw move,
From unda dat plum tree,
Barry madda wondering
Whey Barry coulda be.
Barry getting tired, bwoy,
Of sittin' in dat tree.

An Barry dis realise
Him neva know before,
Sey de tree did full o' black ants
But now im know fe sure.
For some begin fe bite im, bwoy,
Den more, an more, an more.

De bull lay down fe wait it out,
Barry mek a jump,
De bag o' plum drop out de tree
An Barry hear a thump.
By early de nex' mawnin', bwoy,
Dat bull gwine have a lump.

De plum so frighten dat po' bull
Im start fe run too late,
Im a gallop afta Barry
But Barry jump de gate.
De bull jus' stamp im foot, bwoy,
Im yeye dem full o' hate.

When Barry ketch a im yard,
What a state im in!
Im los' im bag, im clothes mud up,
An mud deh pon im chin.
An whey de black ants bite im
Feba bull-frog skin.

Barry fada spank im,
Im mada sey im sin,
Barry sista scold im
But Barry only grin,
For Barry brother shake im head
An sey, 'Barry, yuh win!'

Valerie Bloom
Jamaica/U.K.

I'd Like to Squeeze

I'd like to squeeze this round world
into a new shape

I'd like to squeeze this round world
like a tube of toothpaste

I'd like to squeeze this round world
fair and square

I'd like to squeeze it and squeeze it
till everybody had an equal share

John Agard
Guyana/U.K.

At School Today

A learned fool? God save us!
The pigs are wearing pearls.

Kassia
9th Century A.D.
Translated by P. Diehl
Greece

A load of books
does not equal one good teacher.

traditional
Translated by H. Hart
China

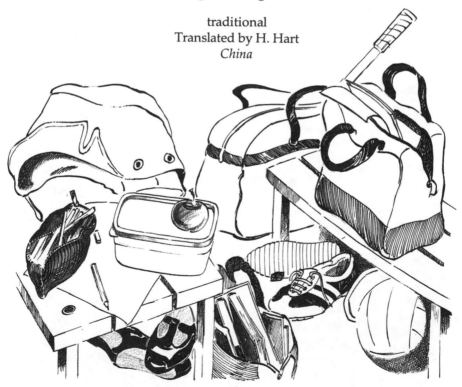

42

School on Thursday

Every Thursday at six o'clock,
I get up and have a wash,
   Put on my uniform,
Get my swimming things,
Check the time,
Oh – it's a quarter to nine.
Off to school in a car
Because my home is very far,
Have the register called
Quietly and quickly,
Then we go in to Assembly.
Out to have a quick game of marbles,
This is my lucky day,
   I hit! I hit!
Go to Mrs. Bell to have music
About John Barleycorn,
Swimming, splashing in the water,
   Get dressed,
School dinner, pork today
Eat it up, that's the way
Maths with shapes,
   Spelling too,
What a busy day at school.

Accabre Huntley*
U.K.

Daydreamer

'Aljenard, Winston, Frederick,
Spencer, wha ya look out the winda sa?'
'Me alook pun the nice green grass!'
'But why do you look apun the nice green grass?'
'Me na no!'

'Aljenard, Winston, Frederick Spencer,
wha are ya look out the winda sa?'
'Me alook pun the bright blue sky!'
'But why do you look apun the bright blue sky?'
'Me na no!'

'Aljenard, Winston, Frederick,
Spencer, what are ya look out the winda sa?'
'Me alook pun the hummin burd!'
'But why do you look apun the hummin burd?'
'Me na no!'

'Aljenard, Winston, Frederick,
Spencer, what are you look out the winda sa?'
'Me alook apun the glistening sun!'
'But why you look apun the glistening sun?'
'Me na no!'

'Aljenard, Winston, Frederick,
Spencer, wha are you look out the winda sa?'
'Me a try to feel the nice warm eir!'
'But why do you try to feel the nice warm eir?'

'Cause me a daydreamer!'

David Durham*
U.K.

44

Daydream

Pen in my hand,
questions on the board
what do I do?
Oh lord!
'What's the answer?'
I ask Tracey.
'I don't know
I was copying you!'
she replies.
The teacher, droning
on and on,
he fades,
my mind wanders
to where
King Fuer, king fu's
and jumbo jets soar.
Where water flows
with blood
and sharks
devour ice cream.
Pictures melt as the
droning returns.
'What's wrong?'
teacher asks,
'nothing'
I reply.

Deepak Kalha*
U.K.

Complaint

The teachers all sit in the staffroom.
The teachers all drink tea.
The teachers all smoke cigarettes
As cosy as can be.

We have to go out at playtime
Unless we bring a note
Or it's tipping down with rain
Or we haven't got a coat.

We have to go out at playtime
Whether we like it or not.
And freeze to death if it's freezing
And boil to death if it's hot.

The teachers can sit in the staffroom
And have a cosy chat.
We have to go out at playtime;
Where's the fairness in that?   Allan Ahlberg *U.K.*

Divide and School

My teacher is like a battle tank
Roaring at the enemy
The enemy is us
And the roaring is the lessons.
He keeps us in a prison camp
Torturing us each day
And he will keep on torturing us
Till our minds are worn away.   Roderick* *U.K.*

47

from **A Bully and his Victim**

A bully, a person who picks on others weaker
A bully who swears and shouts.
A bully who after his fight,
Walks home his face lit up.
Got some money in his pocket.
Just beaten up teacher's pet.
Pleased with himself.

Ambar Lone*
Pakistan/U.K.

The School of Music

I come to school, there is music from
   human mouths and hands.
They play hop
To escape from school.
Tom throws a piece of chalk
   and Henry throws it back.
Henry throws it and it misses
   So he throws it again.
That is called the throwing brigade,
The name is given by a good teacher,
Going grey.

Vivian Usherwood*
U.K.

Mr. Peck's Class

It was the end
  of playtime.
    And all the
      classes
        went in.
          Except
            Mr. Peck's
              class.
                Mr. Peck
                  said that
                    they couldn't
                      line up properly
                      SO

They had
  to walk
    sixteen
      times
        to and
          fro
            from
              the
                Gym.

My legs
  are killing
    me.

Marisa Horsford*
U.K.

Maths

What do you minus,
and from where?
I ask my teacher,
but he don't care.

Ten cubic metres
in square roots,
Or how many toes
go in nine boots?

Change ten decimals
to a fraction
AaaaaaaaaaaaaaaahhhhhhhhhhhhhhH!
is my reaction.

Deepak Kahla*
U.K.

Rabbits

That one and one make two
Is a rule for me and you;
But rabbits never go to school
And so they just ignore the rule.

Frank Collymore
Barbados

If I for one second think
of Professor Deadwright's grammar,
straight away my tongue grows thick
and I start to spit and stammer.

Lucius
1st Century A.D.
Translated by R. Skelton
Greece

On the Vowels

We are little airy creatures
All of different voice and features;
One of us in glass is set,
One of us you'll find in jet.
T'other you may see in tin,
And the fourth a box within.
If the fifth you should pursue,
It can never fly from you.

Jonathan Swift
Ireland

Holidays

The boy's hand
Catching the fish in the mountain stream
would like
to forget for ever

how the pen
must be held
in order

to spell

mountain stream.

Hans-Jürgen Heise
Translated by E. Osers
Germany

Exercise Book

Two and two four
four and four eight
eight and eight sixteen . . .
Once again! says the master
Two and two four
four and four eight
eight and eight sixteen.
But look! the lyre-bird
high on the wing
the child sees it
the child hears it
the child calls it
Save me
play with me
bird!
So the bird alights
and plays with the child
Two and two four . . .
Once again! says the master
and the child plays
and the bird plays too . . .
Four and four eight
eight and eight sixteen
and twice sixteen makes what?
Twice sixteen makes nothing
least of all thirty-two
anyhow
and off they go.
For the child has hidden
the bird in his desk

and all the children
hear its song
and all the children
hear the music
and eight and eight in their turn
off they go
and four and four and two and two
in their turn fade away
but one and one make neither one nor two
but one by one off they go.
And the lyre-bird sings
And the master shouts
When you've quite finished playing the fool!
But all the children
are listening to the music
and the walls of the classroom
quietly crumble.
The windowpanes turn
once more to sand
the ink is sea
the desk is trees
the chalk is cliffs
and the quill pen
a bird again.

Jacques Prévert
Translated by Paul Dehn
France

The Drawing on the Blackboard

The rooster is captured
in a cage of chalk;
its bright plumage is stiff
as my dad's starched shirts.
He will have to keep his pose
until he is rubbed off the board
then, in tiny powder flakes
he flutters to the floor.

Elizabeth Davies*
Australiu

Childhood Memory

A drab and chilling afternoon
in winter. The class
is studying. Monotony
of rain outside the glass.

The classroom. A chart
shows a fugitive Cain
and Abel dead
beside a crimson stain.

In a sonorous, hollow tune
the master thunders, an old man,
shabby, lean and dry,
holding a book in his hand.
And a whole chorus of children
begin to chant the lesson:
a hundred squared, ten thousand,
a thousand squared, one million.

A drab and chilling afternoon
in winter. The class
is studying. Monotony
of rain outside the glass.

Antonio Machado
Translated by W. Barnstone
Spain

What Fifty Said

When I was young my teachers were the old.
I gave up fire for form till I was cold.
I suffered like a metal being cast.
I went to school to age to learn the past.

Now I am old my teachers are the young.
What can't be moulded must be cracked and sprung.
I strain at lessons fit to start a suture.
I go to school to youth to learn the future.

Robert Frost
U.S.A.

Wild Life

Huge bulk of elephant with pointed tusk all armed,
When tiger threatens shrinks away alarmed!

from the Tirukkural
Translated by G.U. Pope
India

When the hunter comes from the bush carrying mushrooms,
he is not asked for news of his hunting.

from the Ashanti
Translated by R.S. Rattray
West Africa

Before the Hunt

Howling wind,
  hear me,
Dancing trees,
  hail me,
Cooling breeze,
  calm me,
Guiding sky
  light my
way through the bush.
  As the stars
protect the lonely moon
  So may I
escape the snares
  in this living forest
  As the cat
stalks its prey
So may I
Be first to spy my game
  Living forest hear me
Chilling wind still my heart
Teasing shadows smile with me
Lead me to my hunt.

Lari Williams
Nigeria

Egrets

Once as I travelled through a quiet evening,
I saw a pool, jet-black and mirror-still.
Beyond, the slender paperbarks stood crowding;
each on its own white image looked its fill,
and nothing moved but thirty egrets wading –
thirty egrets in a quiet evening.

Once in a lifetime, lovely past believing,
your lucky eyes may light on such a pool.
As though for many years I had been waiting,
I watched in silence, till my heart was full
of clear dark water, and white trees unmoving,
and, whiter yet, those thirty egrets wading.

Judith Wright
Australia

Hedgehog

Suddenly, a dark amorphous
Shape in the middle of the road
Drowned in the splashed circle of the
Lamps. I stop the car and get out.

Some of his prickles look dry, their
Points bent or broken. Tiny dark
Lice glitter at their roots. A globe
Of weight and some warmth; pressed, a ball

Of agony balanced on nails
In my palms. I turn him over.
A dark eye flickers in the lights,
Then lids out. Put him in the boot.

I drive home. Placed on the dew-soaked grass,
He lies still as a coprolite.
Twenty-five minutes of silence.
And stillness and muteness and cold.
Then go in for an overcoat.

But when I come back he has gone
Off into the fragrant hedges of
Hawthorn and fallen leaves. I search
The garden with a torch. Nothing.

And I would give the hand that holds
This pen to know what fierce blaze of
Purpose took him off into the
Inscrutable, earthy dark.

Roy Holland
U.K.

Afternoon

Gazelles poise on a silver edge to drink
Shattering the stillness with uneasy sound
Startled far below the unruffled waters
Blue gazelles echo their fear in soundless flight.

Ahmet Hasim
Translated by N. Menemencioglu
Turkey

Off the sharp point
Of a fisherman's arrow
I heard the cry
Of a wild cuckoo.

Matsuo Basho
Translated by N. Yuasa
Japan

The Ground

Ants
are dragging a wing of a butterfly –
See!
it is like a yacht.

Tatsuji Miyoshi
Translated by I. Kono
Japan

Mosquitoes

They are born in the swamps of sleeplessness.
They are vicious blackness which wings about.
Little frail vampires
miniature dragonflies,
small picadors
with the devil's own sting.

José Emilio Pacheco
Translated by A. Reid
Mexico

from The Lion

A great lion came from the distances.
It was huge as silence is,
it was thirsty, it was after blood,
and behind its posturing
it had fire, as a house has,
it burned like a mountain of Osorno.

Pablo Neruda
Translated by N. Tarn
Chile

Hot Day

The sheep lie spread in mid-day slumbers
  And drizzling heat encumbers
  The motion of the clouds:
No cloud moves, no wind shouts
  In the mumbling noon.

  Molten heat shivers on the space,
  The white egrets make pace,
  The purple starlings sing:
Their shoulders roll, their cries ring
  In the mumbling noon.

Kwesi Brew
Ghana

from **Leopard**

Caught therefore in this careful cage of glint, rock,

water ringing the islands'
doubt, his

terror dares
not blink. A nervous tick –

like itch picks
at the corners of his

lips. The lean flanks quick
and quiver until the

tension cracks his
ribs. If he could only

strike or trigger
off his fury. But cunning

cold bars break his
rage, and stretched to strike

his stretched claws strike
no glory.

Edward Kamau Brathwaite
Barbados

Sensemaya: A Chant For Killing A Snake

Mayombe-bombe-mayombe!
Mayombe-bombe-mayombe!
Mayombe-bombe-mayombe!

The snake has eyes of glass;
the snake comes and coils itself round a pole;
with eyes of glass, round a pole,
with his eyes of glass.
The snake walks without legs;
the snake hides in the grass;
walking he hides in the grass
walking without legs.

Mayombe-bombe-mayombe!
Mayombe-bombe-mayombe!
Mayombe-bombe-mayombe!

If you hit him with an axe he will die.
Hit him hard!
Do not hit him with your foot, he will bite,
do not hit him with your foot, he is going away!

Sensemaya, the snake,
Sensemaya.
Sensemaya, with his eyes,
Sensemaya.
Sensemaya, with his tongue,
Sensemaya.
Sensemaya, with his mouth,
Sensemaya – .

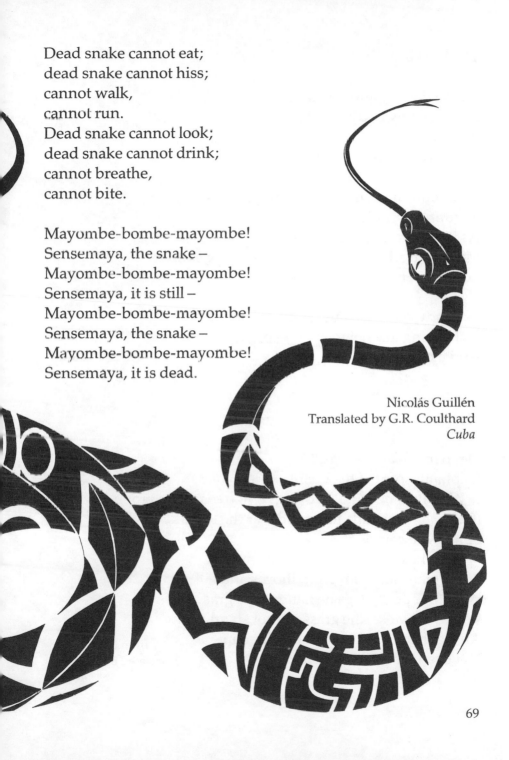

Dead snake cannot eat;
dead snake cannot hiss;
cannot walk,
cannot run.
Dead snake cannot look;
dead snake cannot drink;
cannot breathe,
cannot bite.

Mayombe-bombe-mayombe!
Sensemaya, the snake –
Mayombe-bombe-mayombe!
Sensemaya, it is still –
Mayombe-bombe-mayombe!
Sensemaya, the snake –
Mayombe-bombe-mayombe!
Sensemaya, it is dead.

Nicolás Guillén
Translated by G.R. Coulthard
Cuba

69

The Snake

The snake was approaching,
Its long slimy body uncoiling,
Its tongue sticking out
Like an arrow ready to strike.

Its sinuous movements like hungry eels
Writhing, writhing,
As it slithers through the grass
Make its freckled pattern and glistening skin
Look like silk.

Its beady eyes are never shut,
Just staring like newborn sheep;
And like a river flowing.

Sharon*
Jamaica

Elephant

Elephant, death-bringer!
Elephant, spirit of the bush!
  With his one hand he brings two trees to the ground.
If he had two hands he would tear the sky like an old rag.
Spirit who eats dog!
Spirit who eats ram!
Spirit who eats palm-fruit, thorns and all!
With four pestle-legs he flattens the grass,
Where he walks, the grass cannot stand again.
An elephant is no load for an old man –
Not even for a young man!

from the Yoruba
Translated by U. Beier
Nigeria

70

Polar Bear

I saw a polar bear
on an ice drift.
He seemed harmless as a dog,
who comes running towards you,
wagging his tail.
But so much
did he want to get at me
that when I jumped aside
he went spinning on the ice.
We played this game of tag
from morning until dusk.
But then at last, I tired him out,
and ran my spear into his side.

Iglukik Eskimo
Translated by T. Lowenstein
Canada

We are tired of the bush;
There are no shadows in it,
There are no shadows in it, mind you,
There are no shadows of game.

From the Ambo
Translated by R. Finnegan
East Africa

Water Water Everywhere

When you travel by boat,
Be prepared for a ducking.

traditional
Translated by H. Hart
China

A swan flew over the shifting field,
and came flying home without wings.
Answer: A ship at sea.

traditional
Collected by Vasco Popa
Translated by A. Pennington
Yugoslavia

from **Rain in the Pine Wood**

Listen. Rain falls
From the scattered clouds.
Rain falls on the tamarisks
Briny and parched,
Rain falls on the pine trees
Scaly and bristling,
Rain falls on the myrtles –

Gabriele D'Annunzio
Translated by L. Rabay
Italy

Haiku

I like the sound
of rain; how I long to hear
    the sound of dew!

With the first rain
the snails come out to roam
    like children at a fiesta.

Anton Buttigieg
Translated by F. Ebejer
Maltu

Rain Magic

Gentle breeze is the father of rain.
Soft wind is the father of cloudburst.
Rain will not drench me today;
Rain will pack its belongings and go away.
    The antelope is humming,
    the buffalo is grumbling,
    the pigs grunts in its belly.
Words have angered the red monkey,
but today he has given the right words
and his anger will disappear.

from the Yoruba
Translated by U. Beier
Nigeria

WHEN
on a schoolday
I wake to
see
clouds of sky
full of water
I cross my
fingers
RIGHT AWAY
and pray
for the sun
to
PLEASE stay
AWAY and let
it rain
today,
with no big-
people around
to shout
'boy get inside
before you get
wet'
When on a school
day, i like
rain
best,
So come on
cloud unload
yr water
fillup the
gutter, nothing
I like better

than Splishing
and Splashing
in rainy weather
   TO
make boats from
big leaves
match-sticks
old boards
and pieces of
wood
put them in the
water and watch
them run
under bridges
round corners
throwing bricks
to make them

spin 'roun
no matter if
they go down
plenty more
where they come
from
   SO
come on cloud
unload, fill the
gutter, if it
floods so much
the better, we'll
turn an ole car
roof over
captain and crew
poling down the
avenue river,
COME ON cloud
DON'T let me
down, let the
rain borrow
today from the
sun, let it tumble
down, just for fun
PLEASE.

Marc Matthews
Guyana

75

Rain Falling/Sun Shining

Rain falling
Sun shining
devil and he wife
fighting
Rain falling
Sun shining
devil and he wife
fighting

I really hope
that devil wife
win
because them boys –
they too like to
win everything

Grace Nichols
Guyana/U.K.

Rain-Days

This is the time of bittern and egrets:
notches against leaden skies.
This is the time lightning whips,
and thunder cries, rolls, screams,
cracks rods of iron
and rumbles anger against hill and plains.

Stars shudder somewhere,
lost in a sulky sky,
and fireflies dim diamonds
in grove tree limes.

Rain skims a blue grey veil
across the fields and trees
rushing away to river and pond.
Frogs raise a cacophony of passionate pleas
and bedraggled birds swing on wires,
twig and branch.

This is the time to read poetry . . .

Monika Varma
India

Monsoon

Rain, rain, monsoon rain
Burst from sky like lightning down
Break on hillside, break on field,
Break on walkers in the town.

Rain, rain, lash the earth
Nimbly dance with shoes of steel
Leap in rivers, splash the soil
Knock huts over as you reel.

Not like English drizzling
Water trickling through the days
Cast down from self-sodden clouds
Fusing with the city grey.

Rain, rain, monsoon rain
Leave you must but come again.

Savitri Hensman
U.K.

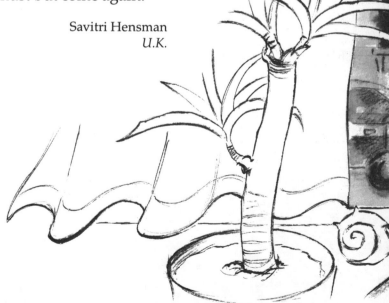

Inside Looking Out

The sky is grey
It's cold outside,
Windows rattle,
Breeze penetrate
Every crevice,
Curtains flutter and
Sway, while raindrops
Beat out rooftop rhythms.

Smoke from chimneys twirl
Forming images that
Disappear in the drizzle;
Dampness creates mists that
Slowly drift.

The street is empty, and
Wet asphalt and dirty pools
Reflect distorted images.

Milton Godfrey
U.K.

The Storm

Without warning a snake of black
cloud rises in the sky.
It hisses as it runs and spreads its hood.
The moon goes out, the mountain is dark.
Far away is heard the shout of the demon.

Up rushes the storm a moment after
Rattling an iron chain in its teeth
The mountain suddenly lifts its
Trunk to the heavens
And the lake roars like a wild beast.

Ashok B. Raha
Translated by Lila Ray
India

Rainbow rainbow
shining high so high
above the great forest
and black clouds
dividing the dark sky

o conqueror
you have poured down
the growling thunder
loud with rage
was he angry with us?

amid black clouds
dividing the dark sky
as the knife cuts the ripe fruit
rainbow   rainbow

the thunder the man-killer
fled like the antelope
before the panther
he fled
rainbow   rainbow

strongbow
of the Great Hunter
who hunts the clouds like a herd
of frightened elephants
rainbow give him our thanks

say DO NOT BE ANGRY
say DO NOT KILL US
for we are full of fear
rainbow tell him.

Pygmy chant
Translated by K. Bosley
West Africa

81

from **On Two Shores**

I love the sand beach of my river
Where the Brahminy ducks nest in the autumn;
Where the reeds flower white all round the bank
And in the winter tarry the ducks that come from strange
    lands,
Slowly the tortoises come to bask in the sun,
In the evenings a fishing smack or two.

Rabindranath Tagore
India

Fisherman Chant

Sister river
Brother river
Mother river
Father river
O life giver
O life taker
O friend river
What have you
in store
for a poor
fisherman
today?

From my boat
I cast my net
to your heart
O friend river
and I hope
you return it
gleaming with silver
O friend river

Sister river
Brother river
Mother river
Father river
O life giver
O life taker
O friend river
what have you
in store
for a poor
fisherman

today?

John Agard
Guyana/U.K.

Flying Fish

Flying fish
flying fish
what is your wish?

In water
you swim
yet like to skim
through wind

Flying fish
flying fish
make up your mind

Are you a bird
inside a fish
or just a fish
dreaming of wings?

John Agard
Guyana/U.K.

The Beach

The beach is a quarter of golden fruit,
a soft ripe melon
sliced to a thick green rind
of jungle growth;
and the sea devours it
with its sharp,
sharp white teeth.

William Hart-Smith
New Zealand

Waking From A Nap On The Beach

Sounds like big
rashers of bacon frying.
I look up from where I'm lying
expecting to see stripes

red and white. My eyes drop shut,
stunned by the sun.
Now the foam is flame, the long
troughs charcoal, but

still it chuckles and it sizzles,
burns and burns, it never gets done.

The sea is that
fat.

May Swenson
U.S.A.

from **Windjammer**

Boat bow cuttin' water
Salt spray flyin' over me head,
Canvas flappin' in de wind
An' lanyard rattlin' ah song.
De mast like two tree growin',
An' de boom swingin' away.
Watch yu arse or yu head gone.
An' is up an down, up an down
In an' out, in an' out,
An' de water makin' green
An' de wave look like mountain
Swish-swishing an' foamin', mutterin'
Like dey makin' conversation,
An' foam all roun de boat like soap
An' ah wish to god ah did stay home.
Who sen' me eh? who sen' me?
No shade on de deck,
Sun bussin' me skin,
Ah bound to peel,
An' me done so black already.
If yu ever catch me puttin' foot
On any kind ah boat again, yu lie.
Is alright for dem sailor an dem,
Eatin' bluggoe an' saltfish,
An' talkin' bout how is ah calm day.
If dis is calm, well, Jesus help,
Ah wouldn't want to see when it rough.
Dem seasick pills don't work neither . . .

Paul Keens-Douglas
Trinidad

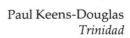

The Fringe Of The Sea

We do not like to awaken
far from the fringe of the sea,
we who live upon small islands.

We like to rise up early,
quick in the agile mornings
and walk out only little distances
to look down at the water,

to know it is swaying near to us
with songs, and tides, and endless boatways,
and undulate patterns and moods.

We want to be able to saunter beside it
slowpaced in burning sunlight,
barearmed, barefoot, bareheaded,

and to stoop down by the shallows
sifting the random water
between assaying fingers
like farmers do with soil,

and to think of turquoise mackerel
turning with consummate grace,
sleek and decorous
and elegant in high blue chambers.

We want to be able to walk out into it,
to work in it,
dive and swim and play in it,

to row and sail
and pilot over its sandless highways,
and to hear
its call and murmurs wherever we may be.

All who have lived upon small islands
want to sleep and awaken
close to the fringe of the sea.

A.L. Hendriks
Jamaica

Sea Timeless Song

Hurricane come
and hurricane go
but sea – sea timeless
sea timeless
sea timeless
sea timeless
sea timeless

Hibiscus bloom
then dry-wither so
but sea timeless
sea timeless
sea timeless
sea timeless
sea timeless

Tourist come
and tourist go
but sea – sea timeless
sea timeless
sea timeless
sea timeless
sea timeless

Grace Nichols
Guyana/U.K.

Of Poets I Speak

The evening rain,
Strand by strand is woven into the thought
of the poet.

Ping Hsin
Translated by J.C. Lin
China

Although a poem is only a little word machine.

Miroslav Holub
Czechoslovakia

How do you write a poem?
start with a word of feeling
end with a word of meaning
dream and breathe-in
the never ending silence
which is always there
behind the noise.

A. Goldsmith*
Australia

91

Shallow Poem

I've thought of a poem.
I carry it carefully,
nervously, in my head,
like a saucer of milk;
in case I should spill some lines
before I can put it down.

Gerda Mayer
Czechoslovakia/U.K.

Try A Poem

Poems may be tasty
    try one for lunch
You might be able to roast them.
Fry them. Scramble them.

Be careful not to burn them.

Karen Hodder*
Australia

Fantastic to feel how my poem grows
while I myself shrink.
It is growing, it takes my place.
It pushes me out of the way.
It throws me out of the nest.
The poem is ready!

Tomas Tranströmer
Translated by G. Harding
Sweden

Empty Head

An idea came
Into my head
So slender
So slight
An idea came
Fleetingly
Fearfully
Came to alight
It wheeled about
Stretched itself out
An idea came
That I wanted to stay
But it brushed my hand
And taking its flight
Through my fingers
Slipped away.

Malick Fall
Senegal

Unfolding Bud

One is amazed
By a water-lily bud
Unfolding
With each passing day,
Taking on a richer colour
And new dimensions.

One is not amazed,
At a first glance,
By a poem,
Which is as tight-closed
As a tiny bud.

Yet one is surprised
To see the poem
Gradually unfolding,
Revealing its rich inner self,
As one reads it
Again
And over again.

Naoshi Koriyama
Japan

94

95

How To Eat A Poem

Don't be polite.
Bite in.
Pick it up with your fingers and lick the juice that may
     run down your chin.
It is ready and ripe now, whenever you are.

You do not need a knife or fork or spoon
or plate or napkin or tablecloth.
For there is no core
or stem
or rind
or pit
or seed
or skin
to throw away.

Eve Merriam
U.S.A.

Modern Poetry

A poem's a poem, man
Keeping in time,
With modern poetry, man
You don't have to rhyme!

No set ways of writing,
Just make up each line,
A poem's a poem, man
You don't have to rhyme.

A poem's a poem,
Just take your time,
Inspiration will come
You don't have to rhyme.

Barbara Zencraft
Jamaica

According to my Mood

I have poetic licence, i WriTe thE way i waNt.
i drop my full stops where i like . . . . .
MY CAPITAL LeteRs go where i liKE,
i order from MY PeN, i verse the way i like (i do my spelling
    write)
Acording to my MOod.
i HAve poetic licence,
i put my comments where i like,,((( ))).
(((my brackets are write((
I REPEAT WHen i likE.
i can't go rong,
i look and i.c.
It's rite.
i REpeat when i liKE. i have
poetic licence!
don't question me????

Benjamin Zephaniah
U.K.

The Dinosaur

This poem is too small, I fear,
   To hold a dinosaur.
I led him here, but he was there,
   And there was always more.

How can I hope to fit the beast
   Within this cage of metre?
He's fifty fathoms long, at least –
   A hamster would be neater.

Edward Lucie-Smith
Jamaica/U.K.

I Am A Poet

Life rushes ahead
with the moon on the breast,
feeling all,
sensing all.

I am a poet
with rhythm and a song,
I am a poet
singing the song of man.

A.S. Amin
Translated by A. Majid
Malaya

I am no poet;
I fight to let words flow,
I struggle to let you, the reader, know
In the best way I can,
Who I am, what I think and what I feel.
I ask only for your patience
And your time,
To share with me
The joys of verse and rhyme.

Faith Barnham*
U.K.

The Pool

Ripples from a stone
    Dropped in a pool
Like a poem's meaning
    Go travelling on.

Ruth Dallas
New Zealand

The Poet To His Readers

Hear, hear this my poem!
Those who do not have any
    Take mine,
Hear this thunder of victory,
    The song of my ancestors:
       My small Spear
       My poem

from the Rutooro
Translated by Ralph Bitamazire
East Africa

Poetry Jump-Up

First performed at
the Brent Poetry Festival, 1985.

Tell me if ah seeing right
Take a look down de street

Words dancin
words dancin
till dey sweat
words like fishes
jumpin out a net
words wild and free
joinin de poetry revelry
words back to back
words belly to belly

Come on everybody
come and join de poetry band
dis is poetry carnival
dis is poetry bacchanal
when inspiration call
take yu pen in yu hand
if yu dont have a pen
take yu pencil in yu hand
if yu dont have a pencil
what the hell
so long de feeling start to swell
just shout de poem out

Words jumpin off de page
tell me if Ah seein right
words like birds
jumpin out a cage
take a look down de street
words shakin dey waist
words shakin dey bum
words wit black skin
words wit white skin
words wit brown skin
words wit no skin at all
words huggin up words
an sayin I want to be a poem today
rhyme or no rhyme
I is a poem today
I mean to have a good time

Words feelin hot hot hot
big words feelin hot hot hot
lil words feelin hot hot hot
even sad words cant help
tappin dey toe
to de riddum of de poetry band

Dis is poetry carnival
dis is poetry bacchanal
so come on everybody
join de celebration
all yu need is plenty perspiration
an a little inspiration
plenty perspiration
an a little inspiration

John Agard
Guyana/U.K.

103

And So To Bed . . .

Sleeping

I would like to
imitate this
countryside
spread out
in its snow shirt

Guiseppe Ungaretti
Translated by C. Wilmer
Italy

104

Silverly

Silverly,
　　Silverly,
Over the
　　Trees
The moon drifts
　　By on a
Runaway
　　Breeze.

Dozily,
　　Dozily,
Deep in her
　　Bed,
A little girl
　　Dreams with the
Moon in her
　　Head.

Dennis Lee
Canada

Glossary of Caribbean Dialect Words

There are several examples of Caribbean dialect poetry in this anthology. This poetry stems from a rich, oral tradition, so the best way to understand it is to read it aloud. What can look difficult at first glance is quite approachable after it has been spoken out loud. Apart from one or two unfamiliar words, it should be perfectly possible for children new to dialect poetry to work it out for themselves. As this is a mainly oral form of language, it is quite common to have different spellings of the same word. First and last letters are often omitted, sometimes denoted by an apostrophe.

ackee – a fruit often eaten with saltfish

ah – I, a

an – and

alook – look, look out

apun, pon – upon

bawl – cry

bawn – born

bluggoe – fish

bout – about

bwoy – boy

calliloo – leaves eaten as spinach

cum – come

dasheen – coco plant

dat – that

de – the

deh – do

dem – them

dey – they

dere – there

dis – this

don' – don't

ear – here

eento – into

fada – father

fe, fi – for, to

gi – give

gwine – going

har – her

im – him, he, his

is – is, it is

ketch – catch

li – little

madda, modder – mother

mawnin – morning

me – my, I, me

mek – make

na – don't

naw – no

neva – never

no – no, know

nuffi – not to

nuting – nothing

ongle – only

ova – over

pickinnini – child

sa – sir

teet – teeth

teng – thank

ting – thing

unda – under

waan, woan – want

weh – what, which

whe, whey – where

wid – with

winda – window

yeye – eyes

yu, yuh, ya – you

List of Poets and Poems by Nationality

The poem numbers in this section refer to the acknowledgements on p. 112.

Africa (East)
Ambo   (1) We are tired of the bush   p 71
Bantu   (2) Paddling Song   p 9

Africa (Southern)
Ralph Bitamazire   (3) The Poet to his Readers   p 101

Africa (West)
Ashanti   (4) Sayings   p 7
            (5) Sayings   p 59
Pygmy   (6) Rainbow   p 81

Australia
Elizabeth Davies*   (7) The Drawing on the Blackboard   p 55
A. Goldsmith*   (8) How do you . . .   p 91
Karen Hodder*   (9) Try a Poem   p 92
Judith Wright   (10) Egrets   p 61

Bahamas
Telcine Turner   (11) Listen   p 6

Bangladesh
Rahman Shamsur   (12) Mother   p 20

Barbados
Edward Kamau Brathwaite   (13) Leopard   p 66
                            (14) Pawpaw   p 36
Frank Collymore   (15) Rabbits   p 50
                    (16) The Butterfly   p 33

Canada
Dennis Lee   (17) Silverly   p 105
Tom Lowenstein   (18) Polar Bear   p 71

Chile
Victor Jara   (19) Luchin   p 13
Pablo Neruda   (20) The Lion   p 64

Acknowledgements

The editor and publisher would like to thank the following copyright-holders for contributing poems to this anthology: 11 Telcine Turner; 14 Edward Kamau Brathwaite; 34, 35, 37, 38 John Agard; 40, 41 Grace Nichols; 58 Valerie Bloom; 89 Mary D. Chauhan; 91 David Durham; 92 Martin Glyn; 93 Milton Godfrey; 96 Marisa Horsford.

We would like to thank those listed below for permission to reproduce poems: 1 from *Oral Literature in Africa* by Ruth Finnegan, Oxford University Press 1970; 3 Harold Ober Associates Inc., New York; 4, 5 from *Ashanti Proverbs* trans. R. S. Rattray, Oxford University Press 1916; 6 trans. Keith Bosley from *And I Dance*, Angus & Robertson (UK) Ltd; 7 from *Once Around the Sun* ed. Brian Thompson, Oxford University Press 1966; 9 from *Someone is Flying Balloons* Jill Heylen and Celia Jellett, Omnibus Books 1983; 10 from *Collected Poems 1942–1970*, Angus & Robertson (UK) Ltd; 13 from *The Arrivants* by Edward Kamau Brathwaite, Oxford University Press 1973; 15, 16 from *Talk of the Tamarinds*, © Frank Collymore; 17 from *Jelly Belly* by Dennis Lee, © Dennis Lee 1983, Blackie & Son Ltd / Angus & Robertson / Macmillan of Canada – A division of Canada Publishing Cooperation; 18 from *Eskimo Poems* by Tom Lowenstein, Allison & Busby Ltd; 19 from *Victor: An Unfinished Song* by Victor Jara, Jonathan Cape Ltd; 20 from *Selected poems* ed. Nathaniel Tarn, trans. Alastair Reid, the Estate of Pablo Neruda / Jonathan Cape Ltd; 21, 22 from *700 Chinese Proverbs* trans. H. Hart, Stanford University Press; 23 from Julia Lin *Modern Chinese Poetry*, University of Washington Press; 24 from *Li Po and Tu Fu* trans. Arthur Cooper © Arthur Cooper 1973, Penguin Books Ltd; 26 from *Although* by Miroslav Holub trans. I. & J. Milner, Jonathan Cape Ltd; 27 from *The Knockabout-Show*, Chatto & Windus, © Gerda Mayer; 28 from *Paroles* Jacques Prévert, © Editions Gallimard, trans. Paul Dehn, © Dehn Enterprises Ltd 2 trans. E. Osers from *Underseas Possessions* and 46 from *April in Nanjangud*, London Magazine Editions; 30 from *Shadows of Laughter*, Longman 1965; 31 trans. P. Diehl from *The Penguin Book of Women Poets* © P. Diehl; 32 from *200 Poems from the Greek* trans. R. Skelton, Methuen & Co.; 36 from *I Din Do Nuttin*, John Agard, The Bodley Head; 39, 42 from *Fat Black Women's Poems* by Grace Nichols, Virago Press 1984 © Grace Nichols; 48 from *Green Leaves and Gold*, Writers Workshop Calcutta 1970; 49 trans. L. Rebay in *Italian Poetry*, ed. L. Rebay 1969, Dover Publications Inc.; 50 trans. Clive Wilmer; 52 from *Selected Poems* by Louise Bennett and 56 from *Native Soul* by Barbara Zencraft, Sangster Book Stores, Jamaica; 54 from *Caribbean Voices* ed. John Figueroa, Evans Brothers Ltd © Andrew Salkey; 57 extract from *Caribbean Proverb Poems* by James Berry from *News for Babylon* ed. James Berry, Chatto & Windus; 60 from *Basho: The Narrow Road to the Deep North and Other Travel Sketches* trans. Nobuyoki Yuara (Penguin Classics 1966) p. 89, © Nobuyoki Yuara 1966, Penguin Books Ltd; 61, 62 from *The Penguin Book of Japanese Verse* trans. G. Bownas and A. Thwaite (The Penguin Poets 1963) p. 146, © G. Bownas and A. Thwaite 1963, Penguin Books Ltd; 63 from *The Christian Science Monitor* 7/13/57, © 1957 The Christian Science Publishing Society; 64 from *An Anthology of Modern Japanese Poetry* ed. & trans. I. Kono and R. Fukuda Kenkyusha Ltd, Tokyo 1957; 65 from *Crosswinds* ed. O. Friggieri, Wilfion Books 1980; 66 from *Modern Malay Verse* selected by O. Rice and A. Majid, Oxford University Press, Kuala Lumpur 1963; 67 from *Hour of the Assasin* by Cecil Rajendra and 97 from *At School Today*, Bogle L'Ouverture Publications Ltd; 68 from *Don't Ask Me How The Time Goes By* trans. A. Reid © 1978 Columbia University Press; 69 from *Day book* by Ruth Dallas, Caxton Press, New Zealand © Ruth Dallas; 70 The Caxton Press, New Zealand; 72, 73 from *Yoruba Poetry* ed. & trans. U. Beier, CUP 1970; 74 Munawar Syed; 75 Palace Publishers; 76 from *Post War Polish Poetry* trans. & ed. Czeslaw Milosz © 1965 Czeslaw Milosz, Doubleday & Company Inc.; 77 from *Poems and Problems* by Vladimir Nabokov, McGraw Hill Book Company; 78 from *The Riddle Book* trans. K. Crossley-Holland, Macmillan, London & Basingstoke; 79 from *French African Verse* trans. & ed. J. Reed and C. Wake, African Writers Series, Heinemann Educational Books, London 1972 © translation John Reed and Clive Wake 1972, first published in French by Présence Africaine, France; 80 from *Stubborn Hope* by Dennis Brutus, African Writers Series, Heinemann Educational Books, London 1979 © Dennis Brutus 1979; 84 from *Tim Tim* by Paul Keens-Douglas; 85 from *The Penguin Book of Turkish Verse*, Penguin Books Ltd 1978, by permission of Nermin Menemencioglu; 86 from *The Elek Book of Oriental Verse* ed. & trans. Keith Bosley, Paul Elek Ltd 1979; 87 from *Please Mrs. Butler* by Allan Ahlberg, Kestrel Books 1983 © 1983 Allan Ahlberg, Penguin Books Ltd; 88 from *Black Eye Chronicles* by Dennis Doyle, Commonplace Workshop 1979; 90 from *Apricot Rhymes* by Dennis Doyle, Commonplace Workshop 1979; 94 from *Flood at the Door*, Centerprise Trust Ltd 1979; 95 from *Poems* by Roy Holland 1973; 98, 99 from *Tall Thoughts* by Deepak Kahla, Basement Writers; 100 from *Awakenings*, Your Own Stuff Press; 101 from *This New Season* ed. Chris Searle, Marion Boyars Publishers Ltd; 102 from *Poems* by Vivian Usherwood, Centerprise Trust Ltd 1972; 103 from *our City* ed. Chris Searle, Young World Books 1984; 105 from *The Poetry of Robert Frost* ed. Edward Connery Lathem © 1928, © 1969 Holt, Rinehart & Winston, © 1956 Robert Frost, Holt, Rinehart & Winston / Jonathan Cape Ltd / The Estate of Robert Frost; 106 from *It Doesn't Always Have to Rhyme* by Eve Merriam © 1964 Eve Merriam. All rights reserved, Marian Reiner for the author; 107 from *When You Grow Up*, Black Child Journal 1982; 108 from *The Collected Poems of Theodore Roethke*, Faber and Faber Ltd / Doubleday & Company Inc.; 109 © 1966 May Swenson; 110 from *The Indian's Book* by Nathalie Curtis, Harper Row 1950, Barbara B. Wedell; 111 from *Frances Densmore and American Indian Music* ed. Charles Hoffmann, Museum of the American Indian; 112, 115 from *The Golden Apple*, Anvil Press Poetry 1980; 114 from *The War Wife* by Keith Bosley, Allison & Busby 1973.

Every effort has been made to reach copyright holders; the publishers would be glad to hear from anyone whose rights they have unknowingly infringed.